T0078086

LIBERTY FINALLY SPEAKS:

THE DISCOVERY OF SELF

A COLLECTION OF POETIC WORKS

DENEEN ANDERSON

Order this book online at www.trafford.com
or email orders@trafford.com

Most Trafford titles are also available at major online book retailers.

Print information available on the last page.

ISBN: 978-1-6987-1181-2 (sc)
ISBN: 978-1-6987-1182-9 (hc)
ISBN: 978-1-6987-1180-5 (e)

Library of Congress Control Number: 2022908265

Cover design by Deneen Anderson
Edited by Julie Husbands: CEO of Kingdom Citizens Network

Spiritual contributions by Lawrence Deon Hill: Author of
Ascension: An Effective Guide to Praying

Literary Coach: Michael Bart Mathews: CEO of The Mathews Entrepreneur Group USA
Author's photos: Zerep Studios: jacksonperez165@gmail.com

All scripture references are from the King James Version (KJV) and
the English Standard Version (ESV) unless otherwise noted

Scripture quotations marked KJV are from the Holy Bible, King James Version
(Authorized Version). First published in 1611. Quoted from the KJV Classic
Reference Bible, Copyright © 1983 by The Zondervan Corporation.

Trafford rev. 06/14/2022

 www.trafford.com
North America & international
toll-free: 844-688-6899 (USA & Canada)
fax: 812 355 4082

CONTENTS

Foreword..ix

Acknowledgments xi

Special Dedication..xiii

Prequel: Time of Isolation 1

Introduction: Why the Title Liberty Finally Speaks?...................7

Section 1: What's Love Got to Do With It?.............15

POEMS: He Is...21

    Love...22

    A Deeper Love 23

    I Can't Go On Without You..........................24

    Love Is God..25

    Without You 26

    You're Loved 27

    Games People Play 28

    All I Want Is Forever....................................29

    I'll Never Be Right 30

    Is It Not There? 31

    When Is Love True?.....................................32

    The Pain Of Love...33

    Never 35

    I Love You 36

If Only You Were Here 37

Emotions 38

They Say…I Say 39

Section 2: Personal Psalms.....................................41

POEMS: Higher Than I 45

DO YOU SEE?... **45**

My Help 46

Why? 47

My Hope 48

My God 49

I Give You Praise 50

Section 3: Laughter: Good Like Medicine 51

POEMS: Gas Station Shefoolery 55

How Can They? 56

That's Chicago!..57

Don't Sleep On Ugly..59

My Flesh & I 60

That's Chicago Too! 62

Section 4: Inspired To Be Me 65

POEMS: A Woman's Worth....................................71

I Am 73

I Am Liberty 74

God Defines Me-Revised......................................75

I'm Encouraged..76

I Wear The Masks..77

Living Saved While Living Single 79

I Just Want To Live For You.................................80

Never Be Bound Again...81

Liberty Revised..83

Just Stand..84

Fearless 86

What Time Is It? 88

Freedom's Cry 89

God Defines Me 90

I Am A Gift 92

I Am Grateful 94

In Your Presence 95

Limitless 96

My Life 98

A Mother's Cry 99

Liberty Revised Again 100

Section 5: Poetic Composition I Kissed My Past Goodbye 101

Conclusion: My Journey to Self-Discovery 105

Self-Discovery Through Salvation 111

About The Author 117

FOREWORD

Sometimes trials and tribulations come to build character. In the period of transformation, molding, framing, and reframing takes place so you can be all that God has called you to be. As you read the heartfelt poetic words from Deneen's past, see how God has set her free in the discovery of her true self. I pray that these poems bless you as they have blessed me. I pray they allow you to see there is freedom in Christ Jesus. In Him, you are free to be your authentic self and walk in your God-given kingdom authority to reign in life as a King!

~ Minister Cassie Reese,
APRN

LIBERTY FINALLY SPEAKS is a sensational read! Deneen Anderson is both gifted and talented. She truly displays the anointing of a scribe. Her poetry draws you into her thoughts allowing you to see and feel her journey to freedom. Deneen does a phenomenal job of reminding us that true freedom can only be obtained through Christ. I highly recommend this book!!

~ Margaret Jones-Jackson,
Executive Pastor,
Realtor

ACKNOWLEDGMENTS

To Elohim my Creator, Yeshua my Savior, and Adonai my Lord, I give all honor, glory, and praise! HALLELUJAH! I finally did it! One of your servants informed me that I would be a writer and author in 1997. Over the years, that initial word was confirmed multiple times. Delayed, but not denied! Thank you for your amazing grace, daily mercies, and patience.

To my children Antwan, Nakeesha, and Darius, my grandchildren (Gabriel, Christopher, Joshua, LJ, & Daryiana), and my godchildren (Zoey, Elicia, & Desirae), for you, I am building a legacy to leave a legacy. You all motivate and inspire me. I love you all to life! My charge to you is this: Whatever I do in life, exceed it greatly!

To my parents, Arthur Anderson and Bertha Kelly, your love is part of the reason I am here. Thank you for your abiding love and unwavering support. To my only biological sister Charlotte, this is for you! I also look forward to authoring your story. To all my nieces, nephews, and the rest of my family, move over and make room! I now add my literary gifts to the family's pool of gifts and talents.

To my church family, Consuming Fire Kingdom Ministries, and all Apostolic Sons and Daughters, thank you for your prayers and words of encouragement. The first of many works is finally here!

To all who prophesied, prayed, encouraged, and repeatedly asked, "When is your book coming?" Thanks for not giving up on me!

Thank you, Coach Michael Bart Mathews, for consistently sharing your knowledge and challenging me. This is only the beginning!

To my spiritual father, Bishop Lawrence Deon Hill, thank you for your patience, wise counsel, and the consistent outpour of your revelatory insights and wisdom. I have grown tremendously under your servant leadership. I am grateful that you allowed me to serve as editor for your first of many writing projects. I look forward to our continued collaborations. The best is yet to come for us both! Who knew that our extensive family history (over 40 years and counting) would lead us to this place? God did and for that I am grateful!

Finally, to my godmother, Kathleen Barclay (rejoicing in the Lord's presence), how I wish you were here to see me now! Thank you for that corner cleaning word over 20 years ago. You were to design my book cover, do my makeup, style my hair, and do my photoshoot for the book release. Now, who will do it? You had me looking fabulous at my 50th! For your labor of love and mentorship, I thank you! Love you, kiss you, mean it in my best Gramie voice!

SPECIAL DEDICATION

This collection of poetic works is dedicated to the unknown man that challenged me years ago to freely express myself.

Crazy man in the store bothering me,
telling me that I am free!
Free to express what I hold inside.
Free to express what makes me laugh and cry.
Free to express words of life & wisdom.
Free to declare God's glory & His righteous kingdom!
Free to express the joys of love & life.
Free to express what causes pain & strife.
Crazy man in the store bothering me,
Call me LIBERTY for I AM FREE.
Free to be who God has called me to be!

LIBERTY FINALLY SPEAKS:

NOW IS THE TIME FOR LIBERTY!

TIME OF ISOLATION

Amidst the emotions of excitement, uncertainty, sadness, and joy she reflects on some of the experiences that have brought her to this place. Interestingly, in her own book of life, one chapter draws to a close and another begins.

Her first memory in life was as a three-year-old. She remembers mama spanked her for something her little sister had done. It was no wonder she felt beaten down most of her life. Now, she smiles for she knows the view of how you start is how you may end up is not completely true. She thanks God Almighty that He knows her end from her beginning.

As her trip down memory lane continued, she recalled sitting alone on the front porch. She was the first to run around the whole block again. As she sat waiting for her friends, she wondered if they let her win so they could have fun without her. As she looked up one end of the street, she noticed the elders sitting on the porch reminiscing about the good old days.

She smiled as she noticed one gentleman had leaned back in his chair and let out a gut-wrenching laugh that shook heaven! That laugh exposed the only two teeth left in his mouth. Sabertooth, no snaggletooth is more like it! Her smile widened as she caught a glimpse of the younger children playing on the sidewalk. Last summer, she was one of them. Look at her now! She can go around the block and play in the streets...until a car comes that is.

Her gaze went upward. Beautiful was the blue sky with just enough cotton candy-looking clouds dotting the sky. Life was not so bad in her not-so-quiet village. As she sat waiting for the others, her thoughts returned to the fact that she often felt alone. Yes, she was a part of a large family and a close community. Yet, she felt isolated. She felt different. She did not feel accepted or appreciated. In her mind, she had no place where she rightfully belonged.

The painful memories intensified as she thought about the adults in her life. Those who should have been mentors and good examples were instead loud, brawlers, quick to use profanity, get drunk, and do "grown folk" stuff that kids should not know and not do. "Do as I say and not as I do" is what they would say when caught in their mess. If that is what "being grown" is, then "grown" is not what she wanted to be. She promised herself that she would never drink alcohol. In her mind, one drink would forever entrap her into the world of alcoholism, or something worse.

She wished she could outrun her own thoughts as she had outrun her friends. She cannot, and so the flood of thoughts continued. This time, as if being played on the big screen in surround sound, she recalled the neighborhood parents telling their children to be smart and responsible like her. There was nothing wrong with that, was there? In her mind, everything was wrong with that! The children teased and belittled her. They ridiculed and ostracized her which caused more separation and isolation.

As the mental channel changes continued through the scenes of her memory, she remembered the name-calling...blacky, dark chocolate, and midnight. Either way, she felt confused, ugly, unworthy, and unlovable! She was teased because of the color of her skin, but her mother and sister were celebrated. They received compliments for their light brown skin and their beautiful hazel-colored eyes. No contacts for them, just naturally beautiful.

The next thought caused her to feel hurt all over again! She recalled going to the movies with her mother and sister, and the gentleman told her she had to pay. Her mother and sister paid nothing. They entered free of charge because of their beautiful eyes! Silently she screamed, "What is wrong with the me you see?"

To add insult to injury, she was often told that she was adopted because of her dark skin and big dark eyes. "Bubbles" is what they would call her as they laughed out loud. It was a term of endearment for them, but a word that caused discomfort for her. They would also tell her she looked like her father as if that was a terrible thing. She had both good and interesting childhood memories of her father, but she did not think looking like him was negative in any way. After all, she was his daughter.

She often felt unloved and unwanted by both sides of her family. Her maternal relatives said questionable things about her paternal relatives and vice versa. She imagined a big question mark over her head because the families were close even before she was born. In fact, Grandma helped raise several of the women who would one day become her aunts.

The stroll down memory lane suddenly became a nightmare! She tried to shut the door to her thoughts, but like a tsunami, they violently flooded in! Still pubescent and premenstrual, he did not have to touch her! He did not have to put his mouth where it did not belong! She never understood how it was her fault. But that is what he said. And he told her if she said anything, no one would believe her. "Tell, and they will take you from your family," he said. She could not imagine being away from her family, so she said nothing. Feeling an intense sense of anger and dread, she conscientiously shifted her thoughts to Grandma.

Grandma was the one bright spot in her murky world. Everybody loved Grandma and Grandma loved everybody. Grandma would hum, sing, cook, pray, go to church, and take everybody with her. Grandma always knew how to make you feel better with kind words and tasty food. Food for the soul and food for the belly. In her eyes, Grandma was perfect except for one flaw. She never understood why Grandma would call her by her first name in front of the neighborhood kids. Mary! Mary! That name gave them something else to tease and taunt her about. Considering everything else, that was insignificant. She loved Grandma and Grandma was the one person in her world that made her feel loved.

There was so much she did not understand. There was even more that she felt she could not do anything about. So, she went through life with two simple principles, keep the peace and be seen and not heard. Yes, "Be seen and not heard" was what the elders would always tell her. "Little girls are to be seen and not heard" was drilled into her. To her, that meant to say nothing but shine in all you do. Her method of managing that information was to be smarter than everyone else. If there was an award for academic achievement, she got it. She even refused to skip a grade so she could continue doing easy work to ensure she got straight A's. What a way to shine! As smart as she was, she failed in life!

Graduated high school in the top 5% of her class, grade A. Shortly after graduation, she was pregnant, grade F. She was told you could not get pregnant the very first time. Obviously, they failed sex education. She gave up a college scholarship and the relationship failed, grade F. As a single mother, she eventually made the best of things by going to work and college part-time, grade A. Three years later, pregnant again, grade F. Not knowing what to do with two children, she did nothing. No work or school, she just sat at home. Besides, she was told a good mother stays home with her children. She was also told that if she had been raised right, she would not have two children with different fathers and not be married. So said the baby daddy who was not supporting his child. Deadbeat!

After three years, she enrolled in school again. She was doing well but soon found herself without childcare. She planned to just quit. Once she explained her dilemma to the school's registrar, she was permitted to bring her two young children to school with her, grade A. With six months to go before obtaining her associate degree, she was pregnant again, grade F. Idiot, stupid, crazy, and glutton for punishment were just some of the negative descriptive words that filled her mind about herself.

Soon to have three children and no husband! That was the straw that broke the camel's back and hers! Feeling guilt, rejected, abandoned, embarrassed, hurt, shame, and defeated she heard a voice say, "DO IT!" "End your life and that will end your pain." "Go ahead, cut your wrists." "Take some pills or jump in front of a moving bus." She shook her head to try and silence that voice. Although she entertained the thoughts of taking her own life, she could not do it. For the sake of her children, she could not and would not do it! Yes, it would end her pain, but it would also end her purpose. She had no solutions to what ailed her, so her inner voice said, "run!" "Run girl run!"

And ran she did! Like Moses fled Egypt, she was out! Like a thief in the night, she took her children out of school, bought one-way bus tickets, and moved west to California. She thought leaving her family, her birth city, and all she had ever known would also leave her troubles behind. Escape and go where no one knew her,

her name, or her pain. She would rewrite her life her way. She was on a bus to a place she had never been. She had no plan and little money. That did not matter. A new city, a new beginning, and a new life are what mattered. Then she heard that voice again, "You cannot outrun yourself, so do it!"

As she traveled with 2.5 kids in tow, the recurring thoughts of mistakes and failures played over and over in her mind. Alone and lonely, she felt destined to live a life of obscurity. From sitting alone on the porch to sitting alone on the bus, she convinced herself that leaving was the only way. She comforted herself with the thought of starting over. This time, things will be different...

WHY THE TITLE LIBERTY
FINALLY SPEAKS?

Although much has been said and written regarding both the natural and spiritual aspects of liberty, I feel compelled to write more. I lived in a city for more than 15 years where the weather was beautiful. My salary afforded me the life I desired, and I had finally begun to experience spiritual, emotional, and financial freedom.

Therefore, it grieved me when I had to return to the city and state where I was born but fled from. Although grieved, I was willing to return as God instructed me to do so. I know it was Him! I no longer appreciated the cold, snowy weather of the Midwest. My salary was decreased by $10,000 a year, and there were so many this is how we do it here rules, I felt trapped and bound all over again. I felt like I had gone back in time. Within days of coming back to the place I vowed I would never live again, my soul silently cried: "I am amazed when I look around and see all the oppression and depression in this so-called land of the free!"

So, now I write to all who are in any form of bondage be it spiritual, emotional, physical, financial, societal, environmental, organizational, geographical, or relational. It is my hope and prayer that after reading and meditating on these written words, you will allow them to come to life both in your spirit and intellect. It is my hope that you grasp a greater understanding of what liberty is. I believe that you cannot effectively use something or benefit from it if you do not know what it is you have. Neither is it useful if you lack an understanding of how it operates or functions.

As both your natural life and spiritual life depend upon the knowledge and understanding of what liberty is, it is imperative that understanding and revelation be attained as early in life as possible. This is important as spiritual bondage occurs first. We are born into this life having a sinful nature that continues throughout life causing physical and emotional bondage until we accept Christ as Savior.

Whether you are spiritual or not, life has a way of showing you just how limited and restricted you are. So, to experience the fullness of salvation and life, you must understand the liberties procured and secured for you. I submit to you that understanding your liberty is no small thing. However, you must understand it so you can live it!

In this generation of what have you done for me or what can you do for me, I am sure your mind is asking, what does understanding liberty do for me? How will it benefit me? Liberty joined with love, truth, and faith will open an innumerable number of doors both spiritually and naturally. Therefore, understanding your liberty and living your liberty is the best thing that you can do for yourself. Sharing your liberty is the best thing you can do for others!

That said, I now speak and write because I recognize and realize that I have not only a voice but a message. That message is, "NOW IS THE TIME FOR LIBERTY!" The whole earth is in travail and anguish due to the degree of bondage (restriction or control by someone or something) that takes away or limits freedom. As the hearts of people grow colder and more wicked, now is the time to awaken unto righteousness. Now is the time to live and operate in your God-given authority. It is time to come out of darkness (deception/death) and into the light (truth/life). It is time to live on purpose through the fulfillment of your God-ordained purpose!

Liberty is an important and valuable gift that is not fully appreciated. Multitudes have suffered and died for the cause of liberty. Our ancestors have died, and others still sacrifice their lives today for the sake of freedom. Most importantly, our Lord and Savior Jesus gave His life to secure the blessing of liberty. That blessing is life! A life that is abundant, victorious, prosperous, and peace-filled both now and to come.

It was through my individual experiences that I also died. Not physically, but mentally and emotionally so that I could be awakened spiritually. The Almighty hand of God delivered, healed, and freed me from my hurt, pain, and failures. My process was a thirty-day journey of fasting, praying, and laying myself on the altar. I allowed God to show me the difference between who I was and who He had created and made me to be.

Lovingly, He walked me through my life back to my childhood. It was there as a little girl that my development (naturally and spiritually) was arrested. I was imprisoned by both real and perceived pain related to rejection, molestation, abandonment, and loss. God showed me how the enemy was attempting to rape me of my identity through fear, doubt, and insecurities. All were designed for my demise spiritually, mentally, and physically.

I was a slave to my past and a prisoner of my own mind and emotions. I tried to overcome them by operating in perfectionism. I would strive to do everything perfectly so everyone would accept me. However, because I am not perfect, I could not do everything perfectly. Therefore, I was not routinely accepted, acknowledge, or affirmed. As a result, the door remained open for anxiety, rejection, and fear, especially the fear of failure.

I tried to live free, but my repeated mistakes shackled me with intense guilt and condemnation. Why the repeated mistakes? Because I was trying to make rational decisions through the irrationality of my pain. I tried to live life my way most of the time and God's way some of the time. I failed to acknowledge God in all my ways so that He could instruct and lead me. Wow! I am grateful for the love and sovereignty of God.

He knew me even before I entered my mother's womb. He knew I would mess up and miss Him. He knew I would fall short and struggle to get up. He knew I would wallow in stagnation. Yet, He lovingly walked with me through every fall, and He patiently waited for me to acknowledge Him so He could pick me up. He walked with me through my process of deliverance, healing, recovery, and self-discovery. Once He freed me, He commissioned me to free others as He so lovingly did for me. So now, I finally speak: NOW IS THE TIME FOR LIBERTY!

Interestingly, I thought my pain and failures were all about me. Sadly, it is a part of human nature to make all things all about self. However, Sovereign God showed me that it was not just about me. My life and my pain were about His will and His purpose executed through me. My pain was His design. He did not cause it, but He used it to bring me into the discovery of my identity, purpose, and destiny.

What was meant for my demise, God turned it all for my good! Where the enemy sought to steal my identity and destroy my purpose by enslavement, God used my pain to help me discover it again! Not being my authentic self and remaining silent could keep someone else from knowing God and knowing who they are in Him. I no longer want that blood on my hands!

So, to those with broken hearts, trouble in their minds, grief in their souls, or are bound in any way, read the content and context of each poetic work. As you read, discern and experience the emotions that inspired each, and allow Holy Spirit to take you on your own personal journey. Allow Him to enlighten, heal, deliver, and liberate you! Allow Him to reveal the real you!

For those who have already arrived in their place of liberty, read each poetic work, and celebrate my liberty. Remember your process, then share this book with someone you know who is yet bound. Why? NOW IS THE TIME FOR LIBERTY!

Liberty is an ever-evolving process that would take an eternity and an unknown volume of books to fully capture the heart of what it truly is. The meaning of liberty is indeed multifaceted. In fact, freedom and liberty are used interchangeably, but they are uniquely different. With the permission of my spiritual father, Bishop Deon Hill, I share the following divinely given insight concerning freedom and liberty.

Freedom is simply no restrictions or confinement. Freedom is not necessarily liberty because you can become bound again. For instance, the alcoholic can be free from excessive drinking for months to years and then experience a relapse. Once again ending up under the control of alcohol and is bound again. In this example, there was freedom but not liberty.

Liberty is the ultimate freedom! Pause, and think about that... In liberty, there is no more bondage. How so? Because in liberty, you are revived, released, restored, and given dominion over what or who had you bound. In liberty, there is a keen awareness of dominion and the right to rule. In liberty, you also understand your responsibility of staying submitted to the one who liberated you. God, through His Son, Jesus, is the ultimate liberator.

Your beauty, intellect, education, and strength alone will not sustain your liberty. When you fail to remain submitted, you risk becoming bound all over again. You risk repeated episodes of relapse. Sadly, some people are free, but they are not liberated. This is evident by the lack of dominion articulated and demonstrated.

Understand that from the moment you entered the earth realm, your adversary initiated a war against you. He strategically releases schemes and set traps to ensnare you. It is his intent to keep you in a never-ending cycle of bondage. Why? To prevent you from discovering who you were created and destined to be. He does not mind if you look and act like everyone else. He does not want you to stand out. He wants you to fit in. He does not want individuality to be your reality. Know that your adversary will utilize family, friends, strangers, your immediate environment, work, school, the economy, societal norms, and any other willing source or resource to steal, kill, and destroy your divine purpose and destiny.

For me, the road to self-discovery was laden with countless traps and snares. Many of them were difficult to escape because I made the same mistakes over and over. I was moving in and out of freedom like people go in and out of the grand central station! I had not gotten to the place of liberty, my place of dominion. I was not completely nor consistently submitted to my liberator. As a result, my mistakes defined and imprisoned me. The opinions of others limited me. I had no insight concerning my identity or purpose. I was alive but not yet living. I was aging but not necessarily maturing. I was free but not liberated!

Now I ask you, what are your snares? Who or what keeps you bound? Do you know who you are? Do you know why you are here? Are you defining yourself by your past, your mistakes, or your failures? Is your identity based on the things you have or the things you have accomplished? Are you free or liberated? Do you know the One who can liberate you now and eternally? If you do, are you fully and consistently submitted? Answer honestly because, in the TRUTH, there is freedom. "Know the truth, and the truth shall make you free" (St. John 8:32). And remember, freedom leads to liberty!

I am finally free! The enemy, people, and my own thoughts once silenced me. For years, I was convinced that I did not have a voice, and no one wanted to hear my story. That negative thinking is over! Daily, I view myself and my life through the love of Christ. Through every life experience, I fight to fulfill my purpose and maintain my liberty.

Now, read and enjoy each poetic work inspired by actual life events. Each written work represents a portion of my story, and every story has a purpose. Identify and experience the emotions of each written work. Perceive your own resulting emotions and examine where you are or where you would like to be. Then allow yourself to be led to the full discovery or enhancement of your true, authentic self! **LIBERTY FINALLY SPEAKS: NOW IS THE TIME FOR LIBERTY!**

"The Spirit of the Lord is upon me because He has anointed me to preach the gospel to the poor; He has sent me to heal the brokenhearted, to preach deliverance to the captives, and recovering of sight to the blind, to set at liberty those who are oppressed" **(Luke 4:18).**

WHAT'S LOVE GOT TO DO WITH IT?

This was a challenging section for me to write. Why? Because love is so complex. There is so much to say about it. Love is one of the strongest and most important human emotions we have. Regardless of race, gender, dialect, or age, everyone can relate to love. Love is universal, right? Is it really? Especially since love is subjective in that it is based on the feelings, opinions, and experiences of the individual.

For sure, love is an important part of life. It is one of the more popular subjects of many of the songs we have heard over the years and even today. Artists sing about good love, bad love, shared love, selfish love, secret love, the power of love, and all types of love.

What's love got to do with it? Love has everything to do with it! Most people desire to be in a relationship with someone. We are relational beings because our Creator is relational. When there is no human relationship, food, alcohol, drugs, sex, pets, and all types of things become substitute connections.

People kill and are willing to die for what they call love. Wars start and end in the name of love. Love is the subject of many of the greatest stories ever told. Whether it is accepted or not, we are here because of love; God's unconditional, unchanging, and unfailing love! Yes, I said it, and I stand by it!

I recall when I heard the lyrics "What's love got to do with it? What's love but a second-hand emotion." Those words pulled out of the context of the song, fed the negativity of my relationship experiences. They solidified my immature and narrow perspective of love. I used them as an excuse to keep my heart hardened.

Well, if love were just a second-hand emotion, Valentine's Day and Sweetest day would be nothing, right? If love were just a second-hand emotion, weddings would not be so elaborate and expensive, right? If love were just a second-hand emotion, then Christ's suffering and death were also in vain. Well, love is more than a second-hand emotion, and love has everything to do with it. So, here is my story...

Although it happened 25 years ago, I continue to recall this encounter as if it were yesterday. I was living in Sacramento, California. The day was February 14th. It was a bright sunny day. I was rolling in my ride with a high praise song blaring, and my head bopping to the rhythm. As I drove along, I noticed there were couples out strolling, hugging, or holding hands. There was even a couple, in their car, stopped at the red light, in a lip lock that was no doubt sealed tighter than a seal made with gorilla glue!

Like a ton of bricks, it hit me! "It is Valentine's Day!" That thought snatched me from my place of praise like a thief snatching an old lady's purse! Instead of singing praise to the Lord, I was deep in the complaint of my frustration. Although I never opened my mouth, my thoughts were racing like an Olympic track star. "It's Valentine's Day again, and I am still single!" "What's wrong with me?" "I'm educated, I have a career job, my own money, my own car, and based on what I've been told, I am easy on the eyes, so why am I single?" "Why am I still alone?" "Where are my gifts, roses, candy, fancy dinner, and impassioned lip-locks?" "I'll have to take myself out again!" My trip down the rabbit hole was suddenly interrupted...

Like a movie on the big screen, time slowed down. It seemed everything around me went black except for the big white sign on the side of the church that read, "The Greatest Lover of All is God!" In slow motion, the sign moved from the building and was directly in front of my face. Then I heard these words: "I am here. You have never been alone." "I have been with you always." "When you were at your lowest, I was there." "Even when you did not acknowledge me, respond to me, or even thank me, I was there." "I have stayed when others left. I have done what others can't and won't." "My love for you has never changed and never will." "Nothing and no one can separate you from my love."

With those words, I knew it was not just my racing thoughts. It was the Lord speaking! Tears rolled down my face. As I thought about where I was when I left Chicago and all that had happened up to that moment, I began bawling like a baby. I began to conscientiously reflect on all the ways God had repeatedly blessed me. As I recalled how the Lord had rescued me time after time, my inner pain became praise. As I thought about the love and sacrifice of Christ, something broke within me. For the first time in my life, I understood love. Not only did I understand the love of God for me, but I also felt a love for myself that I had never known!

At that moment, my understanding of what love is and what love does was forever changed! At that moment, I came to know the heart of God concerning me in a greater measure. It was at that moment that I realized I was always loved, and I was never alone. I came to understand that neither my past nor current circumstances changed God's love for me. I realized man or no man, relationship or not, I am loved! Above all, I now know what positively affects my relationship with others is my relationship with God and my relationship with myself.

That experience deepened my love for God. It helped me realize that my focus was on the temporary external expressions of love through the sensual and soulish realms. I had missed the internal and eternal love that was unconditional and not dependent upon who I am, what I have, or what I can do. Now, I am aware of the type of love that does not ask, "What have you done for me lately?" This love is guaranteed to remain, to never fail, and to always give me something better than dinner and trinkets. This love will always give me life!

Understanding God's love for me caused me to see myself beyond my mistakes, mess-ups, and misfortunes. Understanding His love awakened me to my value and my worth. Understanding His perfect love brought greater insight as to how love covers sin through forgiveness. Understanding God's love meant I no longer had to settle for the superficial or fake love of others. More importantly, accepting His love began the process for me to accept and love myself.

Seeing myself through the eyes of love caused me to begin to know who I am. It allowed me to know that my greatest asset is not my body. My greatest asset is who I am spiritually! The number of degrees I have, or the size of my bank account does not determine my value and worth. Love enabled me to know who and what defines me. It was this knowledge that inspired me to compose the poem, "God Defines Me."

Knowing who or what defines you is important. Why? Because embedded in the definition is your identity. In other words, how something or someone is defined reveals its identity. It is imperative to understand that your identity and purpose are defined by God, the Creator. Remembering this will ensure that you do not allow others, nor life experiences, to determine who you are or alter your purpose.

Before I allowed God's love to permeate all areas of my life, this was a fight for me. Now, God's love enlightens, encourages, and empowers me. Knowing what He thinks and has said about me keeps me from being dragged down the rabbit hole. When I conscientiously apply His truths, it is through His love that I become confident in who I am.

So, what does love have to do with it? Everything, as it is love that reveals God in you and you in Him. It is through God's love that we know ourselves and are identified by others. Jesus said, "For when you demonstrate the same love I have for you by loving one another, everyone will know that you're my true followers" (St. John 13:35, The Passion Translation). Love is the identifier!

I implore you to come to know yourself through God's love. I encourage you to be known for the way you love not just by the content of your resume, the things you possess, or the way you look. Let love be your primary identifying characteristic.

Through my various experiences of natural and spiritual love, I composed the following poetic works. Actual life encounters inspired each one. Every poem is a test that has written a portion of my testimony. However, it was the "Valentine's Day" encounter that gave life to the meaning and purpose of love. How? Because it gave me life, purpose, and identity! I am grateful for that revelation and the continued maturation that it brings.

Read and enjoy each poetic work. Then examine your life's experiences with love naturally and spiritually. Does your understanding of the purpose and meaning of love align with God's? Does the love you receive, and more importantly the love you give, produce life? Are you identified by your love?

Answer honestly and in full detail. Why? There is a saying, "To thine own self be true." How can you be true to yourself if you do not know yourself? It is love, God's love, and self-love that begins the process of self-discovery.

By this shall all men know that ye are my disciples,
if ye have love one to another.
St. John 13:35

And above all these put on love, which binds
everything together in perfect harmony.
Colossians 3:14

For God so loved the world, that He gave His only begotten Son,
that whosoever believeth in Him should not perish,
but have everlasting life.
St. John 3:16

HE IS

Lover of my soul
and defender of my universe,
He has done for me
what no man has ever done before.

He is my knight in shining armor,
He is everything I need.
He is more than enough,
much more than enough.

He is the joy in my soul,
He puts the smile on my lips.
He is the song in my heart,
and the snap in my fingertips.

He is the dance in my feet,
He is every thought in my mind.
He is the sparkle of my eye,
He is one of a kind.

Author of my destiny,
He brings out the best in me.
He's done what others won't,
given what others can't,
stayed when others left...
Demonstrating HIS LOVE even unto death!

HE IS...

LOVE

A caress that was oh so gentle,
a kiss that was ever so sweet,
the soft whisper of my name, LOVE woke me.

Saying, rise and shine,
there are people to see & places to go,
things to do, and lives to change,
and don't worry, LOVE will be with you.

For you, I'll never leave, never forsake,
so, trust and don't doubt.
Know that LOVE surrounds, empowers,
& strengthens you.

So regardless of the tests you face,
come trial or tribulation,
stand and be strong,
knowing LOVE sustains you.

So if others should fail you,
hurt or reject you,
know that LOVE fills & covers you.

And when there is no one left and nothing else,
even when you don't love yourself,
or whether you are on top and still rising,
or facing what seems to be defeat...
How good to know that LOVE still loves me.

LOVE covers a multitude of faults.
LOVE is not selfish, superficial, or manipulative.
LOVE gives life, builds, & encourages.
LOVE is everlasting...
LOVE IS GOD!

A DEEPER LOVE

Beyond the body and even the mind,
catch me in the spirit for it's there you'll find,
love everlasting and love so real,
love beyond the emotions from most often we feel.

Love that is experienced,
not something that's just heard.
Love that's indescribable,
not explained by mere words.

Love beyond the body & the intellect,
for it is with my spirit
that you must first connect.

For a love that has a beginning,
but an end it does not know,
for this love is beyond the temporary,
it abides and flows from the soul.

I CAN'T GO ON WITHOUT YOU

Whenever I feel alone,
I think of you.
Whenever my days are long,
and nights are too,
that's when I think of you,
then I am made strong.
I think of you,
then I can hold on.
Then I know that,
I can't go on without you.

Whenever the storm clouds rise,
in you, I hide.
Whenever my way seems dark,
you are my light.
That's when I think of you,
you are my peace.
I think of you,
and my mind you ease.
Then I know that,
I can't go on without you.

I think of you,
and joy fills my heart.
I think of you,
and all that you are.
Then I know that,
I can't go on without you.

LOVE IS GOD

LOVE gives & shares
never does it take.

LOVE does not sleep
but is always awake,
to cover, protect, and to provide.

LOVE is humility & meekness,
never displaying ungodly pride.

LOVE is joy,
even in sorrow.
LOVE is hope,
when it seems there's no tomorrow.

LOVE saves, delivers,
liberates, & heals,
comforts, encourages,
strengthens and builds.

LOVE is uncommon,
LOVE is truth.
LOVE never ends,
daily it's renewed.

LOVE is peculiar, unique,
and to most quite odd.

LOVE is life...
LOVE is GOD!

WITHOUT YOU

The sun was shining so brightly,
the wind blowing so lightly,
people laughing,
children playing...
Yet, it was just another day without you.

I thought of you a million times,
the smile on your face,
your gentle touch,
your warm embrace.

I remembered the times
we talked all day,
the times we shared,
the love we made.

Now I lay me down to sleep,
I close my eyes, and it's you I see...

Yet, it is just another night without you.

YOU'RE LOVED

Before the world was framed,
you were called by name.
Filled with His love,
embraced by His grace.
Before the world was made,
in Him your path was laid.
All this was done because you're loved.

Empowered to overcome,
and walk in victory.
Though challenged on every hand,
you'll have perfect peace.
Though the storm clouds rise,
He's with you all the time.
All this was done because you're loved.

Every need supplied,
blessed to succeed.
Chosen as His own,
joint heir to the throne.
Life now is sweet,
in Him you have liberty.
All this was done because you're loved.

It was nothing you could have done,
it's unconditional,
God gave His only Son,
BECAUSE YOU'RE LOVED!

GAMES PEOPLE PLAY

"I need you," he said.
"Can I trust you," she replied?

"I want you," was his answer.
"It's a lie," is what she cried!

Sensing defeat, his lips he did part,
Saying, "I love you with all of my heart."

Searching his eyes, she needed to know,
if sincerity was there, or should she let go.

Wanting so much to have a love that is true,
she accepted his words of "I love you."

As she slowly exhaled and fell into his arms,
right then he knew, she'd succumbed to his charm.

On and on it goes the games people play,
as love, honesty, and commitment have fallen by the way.

ALL I WANT IS FOREVER

Together with you and always in love,
All I want is forever.

You are my Adam & I am your Eve,
All I want is forever.

This love we share in the spirit was conceived,
All I want is forever.

To give all that I am and all I will be,
All I want is forever.

Sharing with you the good & the bad,
All I want is forever.

Being for you all that you'll need,
All I want is forever.

Thrilled by your touch, encouraged by your words,
All I want is forever.

Secured by your strength, blessed by your presence,
All I want is forever.

Grateful I am for all that we are,
All I want is forever.

I'LL NEVER BE RIGHT

I know I should not love you,
but I do and always will.

I know I should not care so much,
but this is how I feel.

I find myself in love with you
all day and through the night.

If loving you is wrong,
I'm sure I'll never be right.

I've tried so hard to convince myself
what I feel for you is not there.

But the harder I try, the more I know,
for you, I will always care.

I'm here for you whatever you need,
each day and every night.

So, if loving you is wrong,
I'm sure I'll never be right.

IS IT NOT THERE?

Is it not there,
the things you once said.

Is it not there,
the fact you once cared.

Is it not there,
and what has gone wrong?

Is it not there,
the laughter and song.

Is it not there,
the love we once pledged.

Is it not there,
the joy we once shared.

Is it not there,
what once filled your heart?

Is it not there,
and now must we part.

Is it not there,
what used to be.

Is it not there,
the love between you & me?

WHEN IS LOVE TRUE?

When first they met,
they said they both knew,
that their love would last,
and always be true.

He would love her,
she would love him,
they would be one,
until their life's end.

It was oh so perfect,
it would never die.
Then it was revealed,
all was a lie.

She said, "How could you have done this,
you knew my love was true?"
He said, "Baby I'm sorry,
what else can I do?"

With tear-filled eyes,
and a heart filled with pain,
she said, "Bring back my sunshine,
and take away this rain."

He lowered his eyes,
his head he hung low,
not a word was spoken,
no solution did he know.

Their story ended,
and so on it goes,
when is love true?

Indeed, only God knows...

THE PAIN OF LOVE

You asked if I would trust you,
and I said I could.

You asked me to love you,
and I said I would.

Everything you asked of me,
I made sure you received.

Because all that you said to me,
I chose to just believe.

The more I would give to you,
the more that you would take.

Now I often wonder,
if loving you was a mistake.

Love is not supposed to hurt,
it should bring sunshine and not rain.

So, tell me why does loving you,
often cause me pain.

I knew it would not be easy,
I was willing to take the chance.

For I believed we shared real love,
and not just a fleeting romance.

It's hard to escape the pain,
that I feel each night.

It's hard to know what's true.
It's hard to know what's right.

Love is not supposed to hurt,
it brings sunshine and not rain.

So, tell me why does loving you
often cause me pain…

NEVER

Never have I done,
the things I've done with you.

Never have I seen,
the things I've seen with you.

Never have I heard,
the things I've heard from you.

Never have I shared,
the things I've shared with you.

Never have I given,
the way I give to you.

Never have I dreamed,
the way I dream with you.

Never have I trusted,
the way I'm trusting you.

Never have I felt,
the things I feel with you.

Never have I loved,
the way I love with you.

Never will I love again,
the way I'm loving you!

I LOVE YOU

I'm trying to find the words,
so that I can explain,
exactly how I feel about you,
but our language has not a name.

Yes, I tell you I love you,
and of course, it's true,
but I feel that's not enough,
to express what I feel for you.

You mean so much to me,
sometimes it's hard to say.
To simply say I love you,
often seems cliché.

I long for something unique,
something never heard before.
Something that says I love you,
and also so much more.

As of now, I know not the words
to explain my feelings true.
So please believe me
each time you hear me
say the words - I LOVE YOU!

IF ONLY YOU WERE HERE

If only you were here...
I could rise each day,
to the smile on your face,
to the warmth of your touch,
and your warm embrace.

If only you were here...
I could share with you,
all I hold dear,
the good and the bad,
the things I most fear.

If only you were here...
I could conquer the day,
come what may,
I'd have peace of mind,
whether rain or shine.

If only you were here...
The sun would shine brighter,
my days would seem shorter,
my nights would be warmer...

IF ONLY YOU WERE HERE...

EMOTIONS

I have emotions I can't explain,
emotions I try to hide.
They are so very strong,
they run so deep inside.

I have emotions I've never known,
sometimes they feel so right.
Emotions that make me laugh,
and then they make me cry.

I have emotions I've tried to ignore,
their effects I cannot explain.
They bring me so much joy,
and then they bring me pain.

I have emotions I can't express,
their weight often makes me weary.
I cry but none can hear me,
so alone, it feels so eerie.

I have emotions I can't explain,
emotions I try to hide.
Emotions that are so real,
emotions I can't deny.

THEY SAY...I SAY

They say it's never real,
it's all lies and deceit.

They say it's only a mind game,
and that it's never sweet.

They say it ruins your world,
and brings you so much pain.

They say it's just a moment of sunshine,
but years and years of rain.

They say it leaves you broken,
drowning in defeat.

They say it breaks your heart,
and it leaves you weak.

They say so many negative things,
and yes, some may be true.

I say it is worth it all,
as long as I am with you.

LIBERTY FINALLY SPEAKS:

NOW IS THE TIME FOR LIBERTY!

PERSONAL PSALMS

When you hear or read the word Psalm, I am sure the first thought is to think of the bible book of Psalms. In this instance, you would be correct. Several years ago, the ministry I currently attend did a study of the Psalms. Not only did we study the Psalms, but we were given the assignment to write our own personal psalms. The positive impact of that assignment has been long-lasting.

At that time, I was in the last semester of my graduate program for my master's degree in nursing. I was overwhelmed with work, school, and life. I struggled financially because I had to reduce my work hours to part-time to complete the required clinical hours before the end of the semester. I was bent beneath my life's load. As I contemplated quitting, I was given a prophetic word that I would soon have another degree. Encouraged by God's word, I continued to press through. It was through the study of the Psalms that I found relief, gained strength, and became self-aware.

What is a Psalm? It is a sacred song, hymn, or collection of verses sung or recited during Christian or Jewish worship. The Psalms cover the full expression of human experiences and emotions. The Psalms give us a pattern for prayer, praise, and worship. In fact, the heart of the Psalm is about WORSHIP!

Regardless of the depth of despair, the degree of distress, or the height of joy, the most important aspect of the psalm is worship.

To pen a psalm, you do not need a degree in English or journalism. You do not have to be a deep abstract thinker. You just need to be open and honest with yourself and with God, the Father. And that is exactly what I did. Through the Psalms, I prayed, praised, worshipped, and poured out all my complaints to God. In each personal psalm, I expressed my concerns. I released my pain. I expressed my doubts and fears. I cried in distress and pleaded for help. I declared my hope, and I offered my praise. I gave God all my problems to experience His responding power.

Through the writing of the psalms, I realized that although life seemed hard to me, there was nothing too hard for my God. I realized I was blessed regardless of my current circumstances. It was through the reading and writing of the psalms that I fully realized my dependence upon my Creator and Savior.

Through the discovery of my dependence, I was able to recognize that my intense sense of independence was a protective coping mechanism. The fear of rejection caused me to believe the only person I could trust and depend on was me. No matter how much time or energy a situation required, I would not ask for help. I was going to figure it out and get it done. I thought that made me smart, mature, and strong. It did in some ways. In other ways, it set me up for failure and for what I perceived as rejection. It was not rejection. I did not ask for help; therefore, I did not receive the support or assistance that I needed.

Through the writing of the psalms, I was able to identify and accept as a part of my identity the revealed areas of dependence and vulnerability. In truth, no one likes to feel dependent or vulnerable. However, it is a part of our human makeup. We were not created to be alone, and neither were we created to live independent of our Creator.

The individual who says they do not need anyone is a person who has experienced hurt, rejection, betrayal, or operates from an area of pride. Along my journey of self-discovery, I discovered I was once all of those. Because of past hurt and rejection, I determined that I could not and would not depend on anyone. I decided that the only person who could protect my heart was me, and the only one who could help me was me.

That mindset caused me to make decisions without acknowledging God. I made choices without wise counsel. My self-reliance created repeating cycles of bondage and freedom. It created repeated cycles of success followed by failures. It seemed I would move forward only to be pulled backward or end up in a place of stagnation. Those recurring cycles were broken by the love of God and His truths. Surprisingly, independence is seldom viewed as a form of pride. Well, it is when it excludes or disregards God and His will.

The writing of these psalms brought a greater awareness of my limitations. They also allowed me to understand, even more, the infinite nature and authority of Sovereign God. This awareness humbled me to realize that as independent as I am, I will forever be dependent upon God, the Father, and Christ, the Son.

Read my personal psalms and consider the emotions and messages they express. After careful reflection of your own emotions, write your own personal psalms. Open your heart to God and speak honestly to Him. Open and honest self-reflection helps you to discover who and where you are. It also allows the Father opportunities to reveal who He is and all that He has for you.

*Let the word of Christ dwell in you richly in all wisdom,
teaching and admonishing one another in psalms and hymns and
spiritual songs, singing with grace in your hearts to the Lord.*
Colossians 3:16

*Speaking to yourselves in psalms and hymns and spiritual songs,
singing and making melody in your heart to the Lord.*
Ephesians 5:19

HIGHER THAN I

In the mass of this thing called life,
I seek my true existence.

I cry without tears,
I scream but no one hears.

I extend my hand, but there is none to help.
I thought to give up; I thought to give up.

But then…I remembered the Lord, my God.
In Him, is my hope, my strength, and my peace.

Therefore, when my heart is overwhelmed,
lead me to the rock that is higher than I.

DO YOU SEE?

O Lord, my Lord do you see? Do you see?
Why do they keep coming after me?

I run to find safety,
but not to the strong mountains
for I fear they'd fall on me.

And neither do I run to the sea,
for its mouth is too big, and I fear it would swallow me.

For my good, they give me evil and
for my shortcomings, they give me shame.

Faint is my spirit and weary is my soul.
O Lord, my Lord do you see? Do you see?

MY HELP

When surrounded by the enemy, you lift my head.
You direct my paths.

Your instructions move my mountains.
You restrict my enemies.

You ensure my continued victories.
Today goliath falls, never to rise again!

You restore my soul,
You renew my strength.

By your Spirit, I'm reminded of who You are.
By your promises, I'm assured of what You will do.

So, to the hills will I lift my eyes,
for it is there from which comes my help.

All my help comes from the Lord, my Savior, from the Lord,
my God.

WHY?

Why do the heathen rage?
Why are things as they are?

Why do people prefer the bondage of lies,
instead of the truth that liberates?

Why do people impede justice through bias?
Why do they believe and accept opinions over facts?

Why live, killing the future through the repeating of the past?
Why do we live so selfishly and falsely humble?

Sovereign God and Holy King, lest we your creations
continue this road of folly and misfortune,
deliver us now by your love, your truth, and by your Spirit.

Deliver now, O Lord, our Lord; deliver us now!

MY HOPE

I have given my ears, yet no one hears when I call.
I give of what I have, even though my needs are many.

I rescue those in trouble, even when bowed under my own load.
I remember the hurt and the broken, but no one remembers me.

Dry are my eyes, though rivers I cry.
Great is my smile, though heavy is my heart.

Just before I let go and give in to the despairs of life,
my Lord, I remember your word:

Blessed is he whose hope is in the Lord.
So, my hope yet remains in You.

For the plans You have for me are of good and not of evil,
to give me hope, a future, and an expected end.

As the heavens praise thee, so will I sing of thy mercies.
Forever will I make known thy goodness and thy faithfulness,
my Lord, my hope.

MY GOD

I was pinned beneath the weight of my present load.
So great was my sorrow, that I fought to catch each breath.

I thought to pray, but my words escaped me like a bird from the snare.
I was being trampled by my pain & my enemies laughed.

Those who knew me could not help me.
So, out of the depths of my soul I cried, thou are still God.

God who is faithful, God who is able, and forever I will praise you.
Then, You opened my eyes to see beyond the agony within.

You reminded me of your word.
Your unfailing word lifted my soul and brought strength to my body.

The rivers of my eyes dried.
A smile rose upon my face like the sun on a bright and beautiful day.

I rejoice for You are good and Your mercy endures.
Forever, I will sing of your praise.

From life to life and generation to generation,
I will proclaim that you are Holy, and You are the only God, my God!

I GIVE YOU PRAISE

To the creator of the universe and
He who upholds it by the power of His word,
I give you praise!

Unto Him who can do anything but fail,
even using an infidel to reveal His word,
I give you praise!

To Him who uprooted me from the place of my pain,
and planted me in the soil of my growth,
I give you praise!

To Him who waters me daily with His presence, and
nourishes me with His word,
I give you praise!

To Him who opened the eyes of my understanding and
freed me from obscurity,
I give you praise!

Unto Him who matured me, liberated me,
and established my worth even before my birth.

Now, I see it was all purposed for your glory
and the fulfillment of my destiny.

For it all, O Lord, my God, I give you praise!

LAUGHTER: GOOD LIKE MEDICINE

L aughter was not an emotion I readily expressed. I am not sensitive to being tickled, and I was an adult before I could appreciate comedy. It was in my early thirties that my late mentor and godmother asked me, "Do you ever laugh?" My initial and immediate response was, "Of course." However, as I reflected on the question, I recalled being told as a child that I needed to smile and laugh more. I recalled being asked why I was so mean and frowned so much. I recalled having the mindset that life is hard. There is nothing to smile or laugh about.

Well, laughter is a part of our identity. I define identity as the internal, external, spiritual, physical, and psychological characteristics and behaviors that make each of us the individuals that we uniquely are. Life issues once buried that part of my identity. The scars of life suffocated and had almost extinguished the joy of laughter. Then, I had an encounter...

My late mentor asked me to view a comedy show with her. Throughout the show, she would let out gut-busting bursts of laughter. I barely gave a smile. I did not find any of it funny. It was silly, but not funny. After the show, she said, "You have a dry sense of humor." I am forever grateful for what she did next.

She started a conversation with me that peeled back the layers of real and perceived hurts. She exposed my negative thought patterns that were rooted in my negative view of self. She dug deep into the dirt of my despair until she found the source of my dryness. She then reminded me of God's love for me and my worth to Him.

She made me aware of my uniqueness. She painted a picture of beauty and intelligence that awakened parts of me that I had not realized were sound asleep. She reminded me that joy is more than a feeling. She also reminded me that the joy of the Lord is my enduring strength. Guess what? I have been smiling and laughing ever since!

Well, there are times when I hesitate because of the gaps in my teeth. Then there are times when it does not matter. I, too, will give a gut-busting laugh when something is funny. I recall asking my mother why she did not get corrective braces for me as a child. With a perplexed look, she said, "Your teeth did not get like that until you were grown." She was serious, and to her response, I gave a hearty laugh! I have been teased and complimented because of the gaps in my teeth since the first grade! They are beautiful to some and unattractive to others, but either way, they are authentically me! As an adult, I realize that the beauty and sincerity of the smile or laughter go beyond the appearance of the teeth.

So, why is it said that laughter is good like medicine? Depending on the translation, Proverbs 17:22 notes that a cheerful, joyful, or merry heart is good medicine or good like a medicine. We know that medications are used to prevent disease or promote and maintain health. Laughter, too, is known to improve mood and promote health.

Scientific and medical articles note how laughter provokes the release of endorphins (hormones) that make you feel good. Laughter strengthens and boosts the immune system. Laughter is known to reduce pain and stress. Laughter decreases blood sugar levels and increases oxygen flow to both the brain and the heart. It is believed that a good hearty laugh is like doing aerobic exercise. As the United States is considered an obese nation, a mandated policy for daily laughter just might change that! (Laugh out loud)

The point is this: a joyful heart knows that regardless of how complicated life might be, Sovereign God is there to love, protect, and provide. Full persuasion of that truth will enable you to laugh in the face of life's many challenges. You can smile and laugh through the enemy's attempts to oppress or depress you. In times of sorrow, you can still have joy. How? Because your hope and trust are in the God who is always present and does not fail.

To laugh through life's adversities, allow laughter to be a part of your identity. "Then was our mouth filled with laughter, and our tongue with singing then said they among the heathen, The Lord hath done great things for them" (Psalm 126:2). Are you laughing yet? I am, for I know what wonderful things the Lord has done and plans to do with and for me!

Read the following poetic works and laugh out loud (LOL)! Laughter looks good on you, and you will feel better too!

He will yet fill your mouth with laughter
and your lips with shouting.
Job 8:21

All the days of the afflicted are evil,
but the cheerful of heart has a continual feast.
Proverbs 15:15

GAS STATION SHEFOOLERY

"Girrrrlll, you look good enough to eat!"

"They have straitjackets and padded cells
for those who eat human meat."

"Aww boo, why you gotta be so mean?"

"I'm not, Sir, but that's no way to speak to a Queen."
Just say, "hello, you look beautiful today."

To that he threw his hand, to wave her off,
and abruptly walked away.

To add insult to injury another of its kind,
spoke and said, "Boo he's a joke, crazy, and out of his mind."

"But if you roll with me, I promise you'll never have to work.
Yeah, bae, just keep me interested, and you get all the perks."

As she walked away, not a word she said,
but jerk was the word screaming loud in her head!

HOW CAN THEY?

With their mouths confess, profess, & at times seem obsessed,
saying I love the Lord, He is God & King,
He is Lord and ruler of my life.
For God I live, and for God I will die.
Yet, by their lives, you can see it's a lie.

For how can you love God on Sunday,
call in sick on Monday,
curse people out on Tuesday,
too busy for bible class come Wednesday,
not thinking about God by Thursday,
Friday night & you just got paid,
so it's all about the party and the money you made!

Saturday is a possible repeat of the night before,
or you sleep in all day because you just can't take any more.
Then come Sunday with hands upraised,
again they say, "I love the Lord, it's me He saved!"

How can they say, I love God and there is no other,
when with their lives they dishonor Him and disrespect others.

How can they say, it is for God I live,
when so many are in need, but not a helping hand they'll give.

How can they, with their mouths bless God and declare His glory,
then live lives that tell another story...

How can they?

THAT'S CHICAGO!

Like a stick of dynamite, I am ready to explode,
for I've got some emotions that I must unload.

When I look around, I'm amazed at what I see,
the level of oppression & depression in this so-called land of the
free.

People are frustrated, angry, inconsiderate, and all-out rude,
whether it is the crack of dawn, noonday, or midnight always
attitude.

Saying hello, good morning, or how are you mean nothing today.
For it is as if you said, who you looking at, who you talking to,
come on boo, make my day!

Even the birds seldom sing, scavenge, or even hunt.
Instead, they fight in the parking lot over someone's thrown away
lunch.

I've been stopped by the police multiple times for nothing I
could see.
So, when they let me go, without a ticket or having to post bail,
I know that was God's favor & mercy on me.

Every place has problems, at least that's what I've been told.
So, I guess I'm done with my venting,
Nah, I ain't through, reload!

All the hatin' & brothers perpetratin,'
you got a man & is he attentive is the line they be playin.'

Upon approach to your face, they will seldom speak,
but as you walk past, and they see your ass-ets,
how you be, and can I go with you is what they be sayin.'

My sistas, my sistas where have things gone wrong?
All the backbitin' and cat fightin,' can't we all just get along.

And what's with the driving, speeding, and running you over
just so one car they can pass.

What about consideration & common courtesy,
is that too much to ask?

Even the church, man, it ain't the same.
Choirs sing to entertain, and the word of God is spoken
as if to run game.

And for all those who say where they live is all good,
I invite you for just five minutes to my neighborhood.

I know, I know all the city of Chicago is not that bad,
but I'm just sharing with you the experiences I've had.

So that's it, I guess for now I am through,
but stay tuned, I'm sure there will be a part two!

DON'T SLEEP ON UGLY

More than once I've heard it said,
leave the fine ones alone,
and marry ugly instead.

He will work hard to impress,
he'll give you more and not less.

You won't have to worry about where he is,
or if he'll come home,
'cuz he'll be happy that he has someone,
and is no longer alone.

Don't sleep on ugly is what they said.
Where he falls short in looks,
he'll make up with kindness instead.

This may sound strange,
but please consider the change.

Because fine is over-rated but ugly…
please investigate it!

And you will soon see, fine as wine is a waste of time,
but hidden beneath ugly…
just might be the honor, respect, and love you need.

MY FLESH & I

"Um-um-um look at him. He sure is fine!"
"Too fine girl, so don't waste your time."

"But girl…did you see all that body he has!"
"I sure did, but girl I'll pass.

"Hold up & wait a minute! You cannot be for real!"
"Yes, I am, but it's not my will!"

"Not your will! Girl, what on earth are you saying?"
"Baby, one look at him got me praying!"

"Praying he'll pick you over me?"
"No, praying so that I can stay free!"

"Girl you've got issues. Conversating with him is okay."
"Well, actually that depends on what you say."

"Yeah, that's true, and he can talk to me anytime!"
"Oh God, help, please renew my mind!"

"You need to quit. You are doing way too much."
"Father send your Spirit; I need your touch!"

"I'm gone be touched alright! Did you see the size of his hands?"
"Purify my heart, Lord, please help me stand!"

"Look, he's calling us over. Come on girl let's go!"
"Lead me not into temptation, Lord help me say no."

"Well, you can stay here, I'm going to have fun!"
"Lord, deliver me from the hand of the evil one!"

"On and on it goes the struggle between the spirit and the flesh...
Thank God for His grace and mercy, or I'd surely be a hot mess!"

THAT'S CHICAGO TOO!

Well, I'm back for part two to continue my rant.
Although I tried and tried, to keep silent, I just can't.

With all I've seen and all I've been through,
I must share, so I can help you,
avoid the traps and snares of this world we call home,
cuz' at this rate of neglect & disrespect, soon all this gone be gone!

Why do we steal, kill, & destroy,
the lives God has given and things to enjoy?

Civil, social, political & economic unrest,
everywhere you turn, it's nothing but mess.

Why like crabs do we pull each other down?
Why can't we smile, what's with the frown?

Why oh why can't we all get along?
Where oh where has it all gone wrong?

Why us versus them, & you versus me?
What happened to my brother's keeper?
Where's the land of the free?

As I travel from one place & on to the next,
I can't help but find my soul angry & sorely vexed.

It's the have versus the have nots,
either you get or you be got.

People are rude & always with attitude,
foul, derogatory language, and behaviors uncool.

Things have changed & time is moving fast.
At this rate, we gone miss the future
cause we are busy reliving the past.

Blue pill, red pill, what's real, what's true?
How do we tell the difference?
Man, how we supposed to choose?

It's gotten outta' hand.
Few seek to understand.

Cra' cra' seems to be the norm,
folk disrupt the peace & prefer the storm.

Be whatcha like & do whatcha feel,
to each his own
is a top ten song.

Injustice, lawbreakers,
mass corruption & all types of perpetrators.

Separation & division are at an all-time high indeed…
As long as there is no unity,
I'm sure there will be a part three!

**LIBERTY
FINALLY
SPEAKS:**

**NOW IS THE TIME FOR
LIBERTY!**

INSPIRED TO BE ME

This was the most difficult of all sections for me to write. As I sat to write, the accuser started talking. "You are to be seen and not heard remember." "It does not matter who you are." "No one wants to know about your life's struggles." He tried to force me into silence through fear and shame by bringing up my past. He tried to convince me that by sharing my story I would bring unwanted attention to myself. He even said my story is not important enough to be shared.

I am grateful for the Holy Spirit. He is my helper and the revealer of truth. For every lie the enemy spoke, He reminded me of the truth, God's truth concerning me. As He did so, I came to understand that truth can be confrontational. The truth will bring you face-to-face with aspects about yourself that you try hard to keep buried.

It is said that you cannot conquer what you will not confront. I discovered that to be true. I am grateful that Holy Spirit did not allow me to remain buried beneath the lies of the enemy, my past, or the misconceptions about myself. I am grateful those hidden things were exposed so that I could heal. Besides, concealed skeletons have a way of surfacing at the most inopportune times.

I confess that the lies once worked. As previously stated, it was first prophesied to me in 1997 that I would be an author and publish many books. Since then, I have lost count of how many times I have received that prophecy, as well as other prophecies regarding the grace gift of writing given to me. Wow, imagine that! I was muzzled for more than two decades.

It was not because the prophetic words were false. I heard them, but because I did not know my created purpose, I allowed them to lay dormant. I had no idea why I was born. It is not something you really think about or routinely talk about. I had no insight into my spiritual identity. I just knew I was a part of a large family and most of us regularly went to church. I served, I sang, I prayed; yet, I had no real awareness of who I was.

I believed the prophetic words given to me, but because I did not understand my value and worth on the earth, I did not act upon them. I received them and held on to them, but I was not sure what to do with them. Sadly, no matter how many compliments, affirmations, or prophecies I received, it was the negative words that I seemed to rehearse over and over. I lived the negativity first in my mind and then in my actions or lack of actions.

That all began to change when God's love awakened me. I have been developing and growing ever since. The more I learn about Christ, the more I learn about myself. Self-discovery has not come without a fight! Doing what God has given me life to do has not been easy! The accuser (satan) continues his tactics to remind me of my faults and failures. The negativity and rejection of others continue to try and re-imprison me. I consistently arrest and evict my own self-defeating attitudes.

Confronting my erroneous thought patterns was not something I was able to manage on my own. Although I appreciate every word of encouragement from others, it was and is God's word that enables me to tear down negative thought patterns. When I first became aware of what God placed me on the earth to do, the first scriptures I armed myself with were 2 Corinthians 10:4-5: "For the weapons of our warfare are not carnal, but mighty through God to the pulling down of strongholds; Casting down imaginations, and every high thing that exalteth itself against the knowledge of God, and bringing into captivity every thought to the obedience of Christ."

I used those scriptures to fight the raging battles in my mind. Each time a negative thought or past hurt surfaced, I pulled it down. Whenever my mind recalled negative words that others spoke about me, I replaced them with God's word. I conscientiously kept my mind on God. I consistently encouraged myself with God's promises. Even during times when my face was soaked with tears, and my heart was so broken I felt I could not breathe, I cited and recited God's word.

This was a life strategy I learned from King David. 1 Samuel, Chapter 30, notes the historical narrative of how the women and children of King David and his men were taken, and their city burned with fire. It then describes how King David and his men cried until they could not cry anymore. This lets us know that we will experience real and perceived loss, there will be grief and great distress, but there is a proper response.

Verse six states: "And David was greatly distressed; for the people spake of stoning him, because the soul of all the people was grieved, every man for his sons and for his daughters: but David encouraged himself in the Lord his God." Interestingly, he did not focus on his loss or the fact that his own men wanted to kill him! Not only was he encouraged (strengthened) in the Lord, but he also received instructions that resulted in recovery, reconciliation, and great gain for them all! We would all do well to learn and apply this methodology to life's troubles.

Even as I worked to complete this book, I had to reinstitute the practice of encouraging myself in the Lord. It seemed every time I purposed to complete this work, something happened to slow me down and at times stop me. I considered just letting this work continue to sit in its place of flash drive obscurity. God's unfailing promises would not allow me to do so. Delayed but not denied as "There is a time for everything, and a season for every activity under the heavens" (Ecclesiastes 3:1, New International Version). Now is the time for the release of this work because this is "THE TIME FOR LIBERTY!"

That said, when I feel low, lost, hurt, alone, rejected, unloved, unappreciated, uncertain, and obscure, I read, recite, and pray the word of the Lord. I use His word, not mine, as positive affirmations. I allow His word to inspire and motivate me. I remind myself of His love and that I am saved (Ephesians 2:4-5), I am called to do good works (Ephesians 2:10), I can do all things through Christ (Philippians 4:13), and that I am victorious and more than a conqueror (Romans 8:37). My favorite scripture for encouragement is Psalm 27:1: "The Lord is my light and my salvation; whom shall I fear? The Lord is the strength of my life; of whom shall I be afraid?"

After that, I listen, then I write! I encourage myself through writing. Had I kept all the little scraps of paper where I poured out my soul and captured my thoughts from my youth, I would have an entire library of poems and compositions.

It was a challenge to select the poems for this section because I have so many. There are more poetic writings that did not make it into this book than those that did. However, the selected poems address my fight to break free and live free. As you read, you will notice several poems that are similar in that they were revised and revised again. They are indicative of areas where I was free but not yet liberated. They evolved as I evolved and matured.

Life experiences are a summation of choices that either binds us or free us. That is why The Matrix is one of my favorite movie series. The Jason Bourne series is my second favorite. Notice that they both address the fight for identity and freedom. I have watched The Matrix series more times than I can count. Yes, all of them. I find the messages of love, self-identity, purpose, and destiny encouraging, empowering, and liberating!

Although it appears easier to remain obscure and bound, I encourage you to discover not just yourself but your purpose. Discover your voice and your message. Then live to fulfill it! My message to you is, **"NOW IS THE TIME FOR LIBERTY!"**

Read and enjoy the following poetic works. Allow them to encourage and inspire you to love unconditionally, live unselfishly, and be liberated completely!

In the day that I called thou answeredst me,
Thou didst encourage me with strength in my soul.
Psalm 138:3

Therefore encourage one another
and build one another up, just as you are doing.
1 Thessalonians 5:1

A WOMAN'S WORTH

Who can know a woman's worth?
Do you start the measure from the moment of birth?
Or do you go back further to the dawn of time?
What currency do you use dollar, nickel, quarter, or dime?

Who can know a woman's worth?
Is it valued in heaven or counted on earth?
Who can know a woman's worth?
Is it described by pronouns, adjectives, or adverbs?

Who can know a woman's worth?
It's a seemingly simple question.
Or is the answer far too difficult
for our mere English words?

Who can know a woman's worth?
What's the formula for its calculation?
Is it spirit, is it natural, addition, or multiplication?

Who can know a woman's worth?
How much is really known?
Or is this subject a matter of opinion,
so then to each his own.

Who can know a woman's worth?
Is it based on thoughts, feelings, and emotions?
Or is it limited to one's own experiences,
old wives' tales, or mystical notions?

Who can know a woman's worth?
Is it based on how she lived or died?
I suggest to you a woman's worth
by most is not realized!

Who can know a woman's worth?
I submit there is one who knew.
Even before the world was framed,
& before woman was created and given her name.

There is one who has always known
that man would attempt
to give value based on his own...

Own observations & own limitations,
not comprehending the very foundation
upon which her worth is built and sustained,
and it's not her body, fortune, or fame.

So how can we know a woman's worth
beyond what it is we see?
Just look to the hill called Calvary,
and it's there upon the tree.

Demonstrated by this great act of love,
for with words, it's not fully expressed.
A woman's worth is far above rubies,
indeed, her worth is priceless!!!

I AM

Bright as the sun,
mysterious as the night,
proud as the lion...

I AM

Intelligence immeasurable,
comparable to none,
free as the wind...

I AM

Calm as the sea,
fierce when need be,
stronger than diamonds...

I AM

Overflowing with love,
compassionate toward others,
beautiful as silk...

Yes, I AM!

I AM LIBERTY

For I am no longer the little girl wrapped in a woman's body,
doing and saying only those things to be liked and accepted.

I am no longer the scared little girl,
afraid of being left alone,
or being on my own.

I am no longer the hurt little girl,
that has been disappointed by so many others.

I am no longer the guilt-ridden girl tormented by my own failures,
and no longer full of shame because of mistakes I've made.

I AM GOD'S DAUGHTER!
I am fearfully and wonderfully made.
I've been freed from my past and prepared for my future.
I now see and know myself through the eyes of my Heavenly Father.

I am called to do good works!

I AM LIBERTY...

For I am free to be the woman God has called me to be!

GOD DEFINES ME-REVISED

Over & over, I keep having this nightmare.
So, I wake myself 'cause I'm not trying to be there.

Stripping down to a thong in one single move,
making it jump, shake, and clap to an old-school groove.

Bumping & grinding like a pretzel my body twists,
while answering his cries of whose is this!

Passion and pleasure are good and to each his own,
but I'm not trying to be defined by the sound of my moan.

I'm more than the color of my eyes,
or the shape of my hips.

I'm more than the size of my thighs,
or the thickness of my lips.

I am more than the length of my hair,
and the color of my skin.
Even more than whether I'm thick or thin.

So much more than what fills my bra cup,
& for sure much more than the size of my butt.

So, I wake myself again and again,
'cause I refused to be defined by the skills of the bed I'm in.

I am destined for greatness,
loved beyond human measure,
worth far more than a few moments of physical pleasure.

My life has value, honor, and purpose you see,
for it is only God that defines me!

I'M ENCOURAGED

Able to run through troops & leap over walls.
Able to lay hands on the sick and see them recover.

Able to speak to any mountain,
& see it removed and be cast into the sea...
Superman ain't got nothing on me!

I am strong in the Lord and in the power of His might.
I'm able to withstand the storms of life, for it's with faith that I
fight.

There is nothing too hard for my God to work out,
so, I stand on His great promises in the face of any doubt.

I have power over all the power of my enemies.
All thanks are unto God, for in Christ, I have the victory!

I WEAR THE MASKS

Like Jekyll and Hyde…I wear the masks
of the depth of my pain and scars of my past.
The anxiety of my present and the fear of my future,
so don't dare ask me to remove them because I have gotten used to,
the unknown face that I see from day to day,
the saddened eyes, the smirk for a smile,
the generic laugh, and my cookie-cutter style.
It is what it is so for something to change…I don't even ask.
Like Jekyll and Hyde, I wear the masks, I wear the masks.

I wear the masks of what granddaddy, uncle, brother, cousin,
and mama's boyfriend did,
and momma knew, so I thought,
but she turned a blind eye to that truth.
So that thing, that thing, I buried deep in the depths of my soul,
and covered it with my mask so no one would ever know.
At least that's what I told myself, that thing happens all the time.
It is what it is so for that thing to change…
I don't expect it, and I don't even ask.
Like Jekyll and Hyde, I wear the masks, I wear the masks.

I wear the masks of Cover girl, Almay, Black Radiance, and Mac,
then no one can see the bruises on my skin,
and around my eyes that are now blue, purple, and black.
He says, "Baby I love you. I'm sorry…c'mon…you know me."
I think to myself, what kind of love hits me so hard, I see stars,
swelling my eyes to the point I can't blink or hardly see at all.
It is what it is, change to something different, something better
what's that?
An elusive gift for which I don't dare even ask…
So, like Jekyll and Hyde, I wear the masks, I wear the masks.

I wear the masks and each morning I wake,
I look in the mirror to see which face I'll create.
So, I travel in my mind, even search the depths of my soul,
but no matter where I look, I encounter this hole.
This void…unfulfilled, & as deep as a bottomless pit.
And no matter where I turn or what I do,
indescribable emptiness is all I get!
So, I try to hide, and all the while,
I wear my made-up face and my Colgate smile.
They say the best is yet to come.
When, when, I don't even dare to ask…
Like Jekyll and Hyde, I wear the masks, I wear the masks.

LIVING SAVED WHILE LIVING SINGLE

Living saved while living single,
sounds like a TV show or a radio jingle.

And for most a concept quite odd,
'cause just the thought, they say, "man that's too hard!"

But what's so hard about living saved?
For it simply means you've been rescued
and delivered from sin & an eternal grave.

What's so hard about living what's been done?
Christ paid the price for your deliverance from the evil one.

A challenge, I suppose it could very well be,
if your standard of living is all about me.

Not concerned about your relationship with Christ,
you refuse to be subject to anyone
'cause you living your best life.

It's all about you and the choices you make,
You like what you see, gotta have your cake.

Accountable to no one, it's all about doing you.
No real vision or plan, self-gratification is all you pursue.

Well...living saved while living single,
is not a show or a radio jingle.

It's a doable reality for those who believe,
"cause the burden of Christ is light and His yoke...easy.

I JUST WANT TO LIVE FOR YOU

I just want to live for you, live for you.
No more I but only you, living inside.
Where you lead me, I will go,
what you need, Lord, I will do.
I just want to live for you.

I just want to live for you, teach me your ways.
Search me Lord and know my heart,
try me and know my thoughts.
Keep me in your word, my Lord
that I may walk in your ways,
I just want to live for you.

I just want to live for you and speak for you.
I want to be a light for you as I live in you.
Here am I so send me Lord, I will go.
I just want to live for you.

Not my will, but thy will be done.
I surrender my all to you the Holy One.
Have your way, in my life each day...
I just want to live for you.
Lord, I just want to live for you.

NEVER BE BOUND AGAIN

I won't be bound by situations or circumstances.
I won't be bound by incidents, accidents, or happenstances.

I won't be bound by societal, environmental, or governmental opinions and fads.
I won't be bound by the have-nots or what the haves say by now I should have had.

I won't be bound by the world's music, videos, dance moves, or latest style of dress.
I won't be bound by what he said, or she said, or any other chaos, confusion, or mess.

Neither will I be bound by my past, my imperfections,
failures, or the mistakes I've made.
I won't be bound at all, for the cost of my liberty has already been paid.

Paid by the sweat of my ancestors as they were kidnapped and sold for the highest price.
Paid by the skin off their bodies as they were beaten and driven like animals, yet their resolve was to live free in life.

The cost of my liberty has been paid by the suffering of so many long before me,
and ultimately paid by God's love and the shed blood of His Son Jesus, yeah, that indeed saved me!

Saved me from the bondage of this world, pride,
self-righteousness, violence, and hate.
Saved me from destruction and death
as from the table of my enemies lies, I no longer ate.

I also read this, and I know it to be oh so true,
so, I share it with you and now you can know it too.

"And ye shall know the truth and the truth will make you free."
So never be bound again as you live life to fulfill
your God-given purpose and destiny.

NEVER BE BOUND AGAIN!

LIBERTY REVISED

LIBERTY
I AM, healed, delivered, and saved.
From the moment of birth,
given worth in the earth,
given life more abundantly,
power and authority!
Erased is my shame,
I AM GOD'S DAUGHTER and
all of heaven knows me by name.

LIBERTY
I AM, fearfully and wonderfully made.
Blameless, holy, & righteous in Christ.
Bought with the cost of His life,
how great that sacrifice.
I am the work of the Lord's hand,
freed from my past
and prepared for my future,
& no longer condemned
by the words of the accuser.

LIBERTY
I AM, the apple of God's eye,
destined to live and not die!

I AM, free to be who God has created me to be!

JUST STAND

When the enemy comes in like a flood,
choking your seed and seemingly spilling your blood.
When the weapons form & they come against you,
& the evil one says, "this time you're through."
Then up comes the many seeds of doubt,
indicating this is it-there's no way out!
When life seems to have dealt you a bad hand,
Having done all-JUST STAND.

When every tongue seems to speak out against you,
and the spirit of fear says you're alone, God's not near,
He doesn't even hear you.
When it seems your life is filled with guilt & condemnation,
then the enemy speaks & says your sin has caused separation,
between you & your God, so this time you are through,
& you feel so far from God you don't know what to do.
When life seems to have dealt you another bad hand,
Having done all-JUST STAND.

When the money is low, and the bills are due,
& the job you had closed its doors on you.
Then your so-called friends & family too,
closed their eyes, turned their backs,
& no support would they give to you.
Your way seems dark and the path unsure,
your burden so heavy you ask, "Lord how much more."
Then sickness comes and you question why,
& the doctors say, "We're sorry you must prepare to die."
For a miracle you pray, even in your pain,
yet it seems, there is no change.
When life seems to have dealt yet another bad hand,
Having done all-JUST STAND.

Stand and be strong in the Lord and in the power of His might.
Putting on the whole armor of God as this battle you fight.

Put on daily the belt of truth,
to expose every lie the enemy brings to you.

Put on the breastplate of righteousness to safeguard your heart,
for it's often in the seat of your emotions where the enemy tears you
apart.

Then shod your feet with the preparation of the gospel of peace,
spreading the good news of Christ's birth, life,
death, burial, and resurrection to everyone you meet.

Above all, the shield of faith that you must take,
to quench every fiery dart the enemy sends your way.

And since the enemy tries to bring doubt concerning
God's ability to save & deliver His creation,
make sure you put on the helmet of salvation.

And last but definitely not least, take the sword of the Spirit,
which is the infallible word of God,
knowing that not one word He's spoken will fail,
but all will accomplish their part.

So, when the trials come & the storms rage,
remember what you've read here this day.
When life seems to bring what you don't understand,
Having done all-JUST STAND!

FEARLESS

I am...FEARLESS
because I couldn't care less,
about what he said, she said, or they said,
'cause I know for myself what God has said!

He said, "Fear...I have not given you."
"I give power, love, & a mind that is sound,
so, in the face of goliath stand, unyielding, courageous,
do not back down!"

So, His words, I heard, I believed and yes, I received,
for it is Him alone that meets all my needs.

See, in Him, I can run thru troops and leap over walls,
so, every obstruction I face surely shall fall.

Continuously I press, moving forward-not going back,
standing firm on God's word to withstand the enemy's attack.

I am more than a conqueror. Triumphant I stand,
as I tread down the enemy and take back my land.

So, try if you will, to kill me with your lies,
but know they won't work, for by His Spirit...still, I rise!

I rise above every plot, plan, & ploy of the enemy,
for I break through barriers, barriers don't break me!

Therefore, bound again I will never be,
for in Christ I live, move, & have liberty.

Irreparably broken are the chains that once held me,
so...hear me roar, I'm finally free!

Free to be what God alone has ordained,
for His word never fails but forever remains.

In Christ, I stand valiant & victorious!
I overcome by the Blood of the Lamb
and the word of my testimony,
For I am...FEARLESS!!!!!!!

WHAT TIME IS IT?

Time to stop the fightin'
fussin' and cussin'
taking advantage of each other
and still, end up with nothin.'

Time to stop procrastinatin,' perpetratin,' and all the hatin.'
Holding each other down and back
because nothing are you creatin.'

Time to stop the gossipin' backbitin' and all the lies.
Unplug your ears, bridle your tongue, and open your eyes.

Time to stop the game, the hustle, and the focus on getting paid.
Time to now evaluate the mess that is and has been made.

Time to consider what you'll gain and where you'll end up
when all this is through.

Burning in hell or rejoicing in heaven…

The choice is up to you!

FREEDOM'S CRY

I'm amazed when I look around and see,
the degree of bondage & poverty,
hopelessness & helplessness,
agitation & irritation,
frustration & procrastination...

Murder & violence,
foolish talk or deafening silence.

Enrage & outrage,
disease and dis-ease,
all in this so-called land of the free...

So, I tell myself dreaming I must be,
for not one day in jail have I spent,
but it seems behind the bars of society, is where I rent.

Come freedom and rescue me,
I long to live...I long to be free!

GOD DEFINES ME

Over and over, I keep having this nightmare,
so, I wake myself 'cause I'm not trying to be there.

It's all about the body from head to toe,
covered with a little material so more flesh will show.

A push up here & a tuck in there,
paint your face and buy more hair.

You hear it on the radio and see it on TV,
just how society is trying to define me.

So, I wake myself again & again,
'cause I'm not trying to be defined by the body I'm in.

See—I AM GOD'S DAUGHTER,
someone's sister, aunt, niece, cousin, friend, and eventually
someone's wife,
able to receive man's seed conceive and bring forth life.

I've been bought with a price that money could never pay.
My sins have been forgiven and my past erased.

Destined for greatness loved beyond human measure,
worth far more than a few moments of physical pleasure.

Come to know me according to my spirit and my intellect.
Not whether I'm stacked, or my body is perfect.

Clothed in strength and honor, far above rubies I'm priced.
So, you see, this nightmare can in no way become my life.

My life has value, it has purpose you see.
It is only God that defines me!

I AM A GIFT

I AM A GIFT...
But I'm more than a pretty box with a fancy bow tied just right.
More than a trinket given on special occasions,
or when things go wrong and there's been a fight.

I AM A GIFT...
And I am more than that which you pull from a stocking,
out of a bag, or from under a tree.
Much more than that simply given out of obligation or manipulation.
No, I have great value you see.

I AM A GIFT...
For I am much more than that which you pull out of a wallet,
pocket, or even a purse.
For I am blessed and not cursed,
& though you see me last, know that I am first.

I AM A GIFT...
Created in the image and likeness of God Himself.
I am to be respected and cherished,
not neglected and hidden or placed on the back of a shelf.

I AM A GIFT...
For I am to be given willingly,
never to be taken forcibly.
So, before you come to know my body,
know the fullness of my soul and inner capacity.

I AM A GIFT...
Whose attributes and strengths
are to be celebrated and not tolerated,
elevated and never deflated...

I AM A GIFT!!!!!

I AM GRATEFUL

I call,
You answer.

I cry,
You dry my tears.

I hurt,
You comfort me.

In trouble,
You protect me.

When sick,
You heal me.

Afraid,
You assure me.

Confused,
You give me understanding.

In need,
You provide.

In war,
You are my peace.

What shall I render unto for all thy benefits?

I AM GRATEFUL!

IN YOUR PRESENCE

In your presence,
is love unconditional,
joy unspeakable,
a peace that is perfect…
there in your presence.

In your presence,
I am comforted & strengthened,
enlightened & uplifted…
there in your presence.

In your presence,
I see all your power,
your glory & magnificence…
there in your presence.

In your presence
is all that I need,
& all I desire,
therefore, I long to be…
there in your presence.

LIMITLESS

I AM He for which nothing is too hard,
I AM infinite and all-powerful,
Yes, I AM the Lord thy God.
Self-sufficient...self-sustaining
I AM the first and I AM the last.
Is there anything I do not know or cannot do?
To you, beloved, these questions I ask.

I AM He who laid the foundation of the earth,
by the word of my power, I uphold the universe.
I established the land and also the sea,
such that even the wind and waters, they obey me.

I AM the one who set the galaxies' dimensions,
I open heaven like a curtain,
daily capturing your attention.
Though you see and seek to know,
it's yet beyond your human comprehension.
For only I AM Sovereign; I alone know my intentions.

Finite is your mind, so how can you explain
what you cannot fathom,
when I AM able to do exceedingly and abundantly,
far above anything you'd dare ask or even imagine.

What's impossible for you, is possible for me.
For I perform great, unsearchable, and marvelous things.
The earth is mine, and in heaven is my throne.
It is I who cause the unseen to become seen
& the unknown to be made known.

From the brightest of light to the deepest of darkness,
I AM the Lord...I AM LIMITLESS!

I remind you of all these things, not for my own praise to sing.
For the heavens declare my glory,
My life, burial, & resurrection tell my story.

This...it is all a reminder to you,
that in Me, you are limitless too!

You are strong in me and in the power of My might,
able to do all things as you walk by faith and not by sight.
So be not weary for with all spiritual blessings you're blessed,
given power over all the power of your enemies...
YOU, TOO, ARE LIMITLESS!

MY LIFE

Born into sin,
raised in the ghetto,
be seen & not heard,
this is your life.

Go to school,
get good grades,
your dreams may come true,
this is your life.

Work hard for a little,
struggle it makes you strong,
remain silent it's safe,
this is your life.

A slave to this world,
in bondage, you die,
it is what it is,
this is your life.

Not for me this life!
See, I've been bought with a price.
Freed from the curses of poverty, sin, & death,
destined to reign & rule with the Messiah, Christ Himself!

Life more abundantly,
power & authority,
for all eternity…

NOW THAT'S MY LIFE!

A MOTHER'S CRY

With joy, sometimes discomfort, I carried you.
With anxiety & anticipation, I looked forward to your arrival.
In pain, I gave birth to you. With hope, I held you.
In love, I raised you. As an infant, I watched you, fed and protected
you, dreamt of all the possibilities that were ahead, for you.

As you grew, I marveled.
This…how could I have done,
sitting up, crawling, first word, first step…this is my beloved son.
How wonderful, so amazing just how much you needed me,
To teach, support, & guide you, no matter what the need.

Independence soon moved in & slowly I lost my place.
As you developed your own mind, your own dreams,
it seemed all I had given was replaced.

Now, you're all grown up, where are you…I understand not.
For you've walked away from all you were given,
and all you were ever taught.

Lord, please help, protect, and provide,
these are often the words as a mother I've cried.

The pain, uncertainty, the anguish runs so deep,
in prayer I can only go before I close my eyes to sleep.
My Lord, this trial, what have I done to deserve such,
when the child from my womb I have loved so much.
God…please help me…
deliver him, in sin please let him not die!

These are often the words…

AS A MOTHER I'VE CRIED!

LIBERTY REVISED AGAIN

Who are you?
I AM LIBERTY & LIBERTY I AM...
For I am no longer the little girl wrapped in a woman's body,
doing and saying only that which will make me accepted.
No longer guilt-ridden or filled with shame,
because by society I've been rejected.
No longer held down or back because of my failures,
or the mistakes I've made.
No longer deceived and tripped up,
by the traps my enemies have laid.
No longer afraid to be left alone or be on my own,
now I have a brand-new song...

Who are you?
I AM LIBERTY & LIBERTY I AM...
For I am God's daughter, fearfully and wonderfully made,
freed from my past & prepared for my future,
in Christ, my destiny is eternally paved.
I know myself through the eyes of my Heavenly Father.
So how you perceive me and what you think of me,
with that I will not be bothered.

Who are you?
I AM LIBERTY & LIBERTY I AM...
For I am now free to be who & what God has anointed me to be!

I KISSED MY PAST GOODBYE

When I think of your very definition, I cannot help but ask myself why are you still in my present? How is it possible that you, who should be no more, are still affecting me now? Why do I give you time and energy? Why have I allowed you to slow me down, hold me up, and at times, just all-out stop me?

My past, why are you still here? If I could say that your effect was always positive, I may not mind having you around. You have not been all that I wanted, but I have learned a few things. Most importantly, I have learned things about myself, and it is time, now time, that I apply and live what I have learned. I have carried you long enough. I have given you more time than you should have had. I have allowed you to dictate what I do and where I go long enough. Your illegal rule is over, finished, and will be no more, forever!

Interestingly, when I sat to write you this letter, it was my intent to let you have it! I intended to remind you of all the psychological and physical pain you have caused me and those connected to me. It was my intent to list from A to Z all that you have done to imprison me and cause me to grow slowly, move too cautiously, and question who I am and why I was even born.

In fact, I was told I would never get over or past you if I did not confront you. Although I know there is truth to that, I decided that this time, it was not necessary. See, I have confronted you before.

I have named and called you out before. I have cried because of you before, and I have earnestly prayed against you. My parents, mentors, friends, and pastor have prayed against you. Above all, Jesus, my Savior, has already dealt with you. He has already overcome all that is in the world. Likewise, in Him, I overcome you and all that you have caused!

So, my past, I FORGIVE you for all you have done. I FORGIVE myself for all I allowed you to do. Today, I RELEASE you! I release you from your illegal authority, power, and control over my life. I TAKE BACK my identity, my voice, my purpose, and my God-given dominion. I take back every tangible and intangible thing you have stolen, especially my time and resources. I, do, THANK YOU, and appreciate the life lessons.

Today and every day, I shall remind myself of the word of the Lord that admonishes me to stop dwelling on the past and not remember the former things (Isaiah 43:18). Instead, I will live every day focused as I press and reach forward to what is ahead...my future, my God-given future, in Christ (Philippians 3:13).

My past, I remind you that the old has passed away and all is new (2 Corinthians 5:17). I AM A NEW CREATION! I AM WHO GOD SAYS I AM. I am loved, forgiven, healed, made whole, and freed from the shame, guilt, and pain of the past.

Now, by faith, I am securely tied to my abundant future in Christ! I am anointed and appointed as worshipper, prophet, intercessor, teacher, scribe, and servant of the Most High God. I AM WHO GOD SAYS I AM, and I WILL do all He has anointed and appointed me to do!

GOODBYE, my past, GOODBYE! NOW IS MY TIME FOR LIBERTY!

"Brothers, I do not consider that I have made it my own.
But one thing I do: forgetting what lies behind and straining
forward to what lies ahead, I press on toward the goal for
the prize of the upward call of God in Christ Jesus."
Philippians 3:13-14

"Therefore, if anyone is in Christ, he is a
new creation. The old has passed
away; behold, the new has come."
2 Corinthians 5:17

"Remember not the former things, nor consider the things of old."
Isaiah 43:18

LIBERTY FINALLY SPEAKS:

NOW IS THE TIME FOR LIBERTY!

MY JOURNEY TO SELF-DISCOVERY

G ood, bad, or indifferent, we are often the summation and expressions of our lived experiences. I am grateful that regardless of the experiences, you can change your response and point of view if you want. Just like you do not have to be a product of your negative environment, you also do not have to be the summation of your negative life experiences. The memory and impact of the experiences do not have to limit or fully define you. That said, change is not always easy. However, it is an option if you choose to take it. I chose to take it, eventually anyway.

Yes, I finally decided it was time, past time, and long over-due time. I was so tired, my tired was tired of living in bondage as a slave to my past and a prisoner of my own mind. Psychological imprisonment dragged me through life scarring up everything. It even pulled the scab off areas that were in the process of healing. At the rate I was going, it was going to be a life sentence. Arrested and living behind invisible bars without a key or any foreseeable way out!

Thank God, in heaven, for LIBERTY! Now instead of being tired, I am so excited, my excited is excited because I am free! I am free to be who and what God has ordained me to be. I am free to accomplish all that He has purposed for me to accomplish. I am free to be...!

In hindsight, I realize I was free a long time ago, but I somehow allowed select life experiences to imprison me over and over. Life became a cycle of freedom, bondage, freedom then bondage again. I was free but not liberated because I did not have dominion over the things that repeatedly imprisoned me. I did not have dominion over my negative thoughts or the opinions of others. Enough already, right?

Yes, I finally made up my mind. I made the decision to live free and liberated. However, I discovered that freedom is not a fixed position. It is fluid and living, and you must fight for it every day. With each life experience, you must stand firm against the return to any form of bondage. Why? Because if allowed, people and life's daily experiences may detain, delay, or derail you. If allowed, they will place you in bondage all over again.

Through my story, I have shared what once was my life's sentence. What is your sentence? Is that disappointment from one, five, or ten years ago keeping you on lockdown? Did that recent, past, or one-time failure cause you to give up your life's dream? Has that divorce, loss of a loved one, or betrayal caused you to harden your heart? Or are you a lifer, meaning you refuse to let it go? NOW IS THE TIME FOR LIBERTY!

So, how did I become free? First, by believing and accepting that the complete work of Jesus purchased and guarantees my freedom and liberty in all areas of my life. My relationship with Him is what makes and keeps me free. True freedom starts in Christ and is maintained in Him. Without Him as Savior and Lord, you cannot know or experience true freedom. You can only experience what appears to be freedom. Time will reveal the difference.

Secondly, the more I know about Him, the more I know about myself. Life has a way of revealing who you are. It does not matter how you try to cover up or hide flaws, mistakes, or failures with makeup, money, education, cars, alcohol, drugs, sex, or other external things. They are all superficial and provide only temporary satisfaction. Some would say, use those things to fake it until you make it. I say a fake life is no life, and it is still a life of bondage.

I once did a lot of faking. As a result, my life was almost unrealized. Here is how. I was raised primarily by my grandmother and mother. Additionally, multiple aunts greatly influenced me. All strong, intelligent, and independent women. I was often in awe of how they took care of so many of us with little to no help from our fathers. I have great respect for them and appreciate their influence.

However, as stated earlier, it was repeatedly said that little girls were to be seen and not heard. Growing up with that embedded in my mind, silenced my voice. In hindsight, I know it was not said with malice or with intent to harm, but it did. It muted my voice, and it seemed no one around me understood my sign language.

For years, I was quiet and passive. I was so quiet in school; my teachers would call my name just to hear me answer. I was often told, "You need to stop being so nice and stop letting people walk all over you. Well, I was adhering to the instructions of my elders, so I thought. I did not know there were appropriate times to speak up. I did not realize I had the right to confront those who were crushing my spirit and breaking my heart.

So, in silence, I suffered. I wanted to speak up, but I did not know how or when. Therefore, I smiled in public (externally) but cried in private (internally). Introversion became my protection. I even took on the characteristics of a chameleon. I learned to blend into any environment so that I did not draw any attention to myself.

I lived uncomfortably in a place of obscurity. If you did not ask, I did not tell.

As a result, numerous things were unspoken and unaddressed. I was forty years old before I spoke about the sexual and psychological abuse I suffered. When I did disclose it, I encountered hostility. I was told that since I had kept it a secret for all those years, I should have just remained silent. However, I could not. The disclosure was a part of my freedom journey. I imagined myself being choked to unconsciousness by the guilt and shame of trying to keep quiet for the sake of others. If I were not healed in that area of my life, the dismissive reactions of those that I thought would be supportive could have pushed me back behind the invisible bars.

During those times when I was afraid to speak, what I could not say openly, I wrote, prayed, or sang in private. With each word, I peeled off the pain of rejection, the shame of molestation, the anger of manipulation, the guilt of self-condemnation, and the fear of failure. Doing that broke and continues to break the cycles of bondage. Thank God for freedom!

How do I stay free? I stay free through consistent fellowship with my Savior Jesus, through worship, prayer, and serving others. I consistently study and apply God's word to the best of my ability. I keep in mind that everything and everyone around me may change or fail, but God does not change, and He cannot fail.

Thirteen years ago, when I wrote the initial draft for this book, I allowed a good friend (who is now resting in God's presence) to read the initial introduction. After reading it, he asked me a question. He said, "If you knew that you could not fail, what would you do?" It was as if he could see all the thoughts and ideas going through my mind. He then said to me, "Do them! God does not fail, and in Him, you won't either." I did not get it then, but I get it now!

I also know that the journey is not over! I have only completed the current course, and this written work is only the beginning. As I continue to grow in the grace and knowledge of God, learning more about Him and His will, the more I will grow in the knowledge of who I am and what He has called me to be and do.

The journey I once feared, I now embrace. The journey I once misunderstood, I now understand I do not have to know it all. I must trust the One who gave me life and sustains my life. Had it not been for the fires of life, I would not know my divinely created self. I would not know my life's purpose or mandate. I could not live authentically, and I could not confidently declare to you, "NOW IS THE TIME FOR LIBERTY!"

How do I stay free? By wisely using what I consider to be the second greatest gift to humanity. The first is God's unconditional love. The second is the ability to choose. Yes, living free and liberated starts with making the choice to do so. Think about it. We choose who and what we like or dislike. We choose what to wear and what to eat. We choose where to work and where to live. We choose to obey the law or break it. We choose who we will love or hate. We must choose who we will serve, God or man (Joshua 24:15).

My point is this, every day there are choices to make. Therefore, we must choose wisely. What helps me to choose wisely? The aid of the Holy Spirit and the understanding of who I am and what I am called to do. What will help you to choose wisely? I submit to you the same answer: the aid of the Holy Spirit and the understanding of who you are and what you are called to do. Decisions made in alignment with these fundamental truths minimize bondage and ensure freedom regardless of circumstances. It is not easy, but it is well worth it!

My journey to self-discovery has been both challenging and rewarding. It was challenging because of the physical and emotional things I endured. It was the testing of my abilities and the trying of my faith that has fashioned me into the woman I am today. It was rewarding because I now see those experiences from the proper perspective. The pain had a purpose. The good outweighs the bad, and I have had more victories than defeats.

Shifting my focus from my mistakes, failures, pain, and scars helped me realize they were the pathways to my identity and my purpose. Each negative experience became a rung in the ladder that ultimately lifted me over my circumstances. My tests and trials were not designed to imprison me. My choices did that. They were designed to bring me to the place of knowing myself and my purpose through my relationship with Christ. The knowledge of self and purpose allows me to live and share my life's mandate and message: NOW IS THE TIME FOR LIBERTY! Now is the time for YOU to unmask! Now is the time for you to live free and liberated!

That said, I implore you to choose to discover and know your divinely created self and live to fulfill your life's purpose. Now, read on for the conclusion of the whole matter.

SELF-DISCOVERY THROUGH SALVATION

If you are reading this page, it is my hope and prayer that you have read this work in its entirety. Your emotions are stirred, your heart is deeply pricked, and your spirit is loudly crying to be set free! It is in the discovery of self that freedom is birthed. In my opinion, self-discovery has some aspects that are like pregnancy and childbirth. To the men reading this, please keep reading. There is an explanation.

Pregnancy comes with emotional, physical, and psychological changes. There may be weight loss or weight gain, hair loss or growth, swelling, skin changes, and overall changes both inside and outside of the body. All these changes are occurring as the life inside is developing and growing so that at the appointed time, he, or she will come forth as an individual distinct from its original host (the mother).

An individual that does not know his or her divinely created self is like being pregnant. They will outwardly change the style of their hair, nails, and clothes. They will tuck this, push up that, pierce this, paint that, add friends, drop friends, drive this, live there, and go from this to that or that to this. All the while, the inner person (the divinely created self) is longing to be birthed.

There is an ongoing struggle between the inner person and the outer person. In many instances, the birth of the inner person is delayed by the opinions of others, unexpected circumstances, fear, and personal choices. Sadly, in some instances, the inner authentic, divinely created self is never born.

Then there is childbirth. It can be scary, humiliating, painful, exhausting, and it can be life-threatening. However, after it is all over and you take one look at the new life that presents renewed hope and great possibilities, you know it was all worth it!

Likewise with self-discovery. Seeking to know oneself can be challenging (so many unknowns). It can be humbling (due to mistakes and failures) and agonizing (due to being hurt by others or one's own guilt and shame). It can also be exhausting or oppressive (wondering if you will ever make it), and it may lead to giving up because you do not know what else to do or who to turn to for help.

However, after all the pushing, pressing, and prevailing, you are born. The authentically created you can now be developed and further enhanced. You know who you are. You are freed from all that once held you captive. You have dominion over what once had dominion over you. You are confident and living out your purpose. To that you say, it was all worth it!

The way to a life of freedom and liberty is in relationship with God, the Father, through His Son, Jesus. The surest way to live as your authentic self is in a covenant relationship with God through Christ. All else is superficial and temporary. Liberty in Christ is everlasting!

Having read my story, pause here and review, evaluate, examine, and reflect on your own life's story. As you do, keep in mind these important principles that will ensure the discovery of self. First, understand that being delivered or saved from something also denotes being delivered or saved to something. For example, from death to life, from sickness to health, from poverty to wealth, or from born self to divinely created self. Do you follow? Good!

Second, also bear in mind the principle of forgiveness. Forgiveness is important because its opposite is unforgiveness. Unforgiveness opens the door and holds it open for all forms of bondage. Unforgiveness is like ingesting a slow-acting poison that over time, negatively affects you and everything connected to you. Unforgiveness leads to bitterness, resentment, anger, hate, and eventually physical and psychological illnesses.

Therefore, ask Holy Spirit to assist you in implementing the principle of forgiveness in all areas of your life. Ask God to forgive you for all sins known and unknown. This is an important first step. Then forgive those who hurt you, used you, talked about you, rejected you, and did things to you hoping for your demise. This is important because if you do not forgive others, you will not be forgiven (Matthew 6:15). And do not forget to forgive yourself for all your mistakes, failures, and shortcomings. This may be as challenging as forgiving others, but it is also as important. So, forgive to live and move forward.

Last, but not least, love. Yes, love! Remember, love has everything to do with it! What is IT? It is your identity and your purpose. Love is the seed of life! This is not what can you do for me or what have you done for me lately type of love. I am referring to a genuine love for God, others, and yourself. I am referring to love that is rooted in the spirit, and it is not changed or destroyed by the opinions or mood swings of self and others.

This love is clearly spoken and consistently demonstrated. This type of love covers all aspects of life spiritual, natural, physical, and psychological. This love is quick to hear, slow to speak, and quick to forgive. This love covers faults and does not fail. This love gives life!

This is the definition of love I want you to remember from now on: love is willful sacrificial acts of service. In other words, you choose to selflessly serve others. This is the love that God demonstrates and gives to us every day so that we may give the same love to others.

Now, exchange your fears for faith and your despair for hope. Exchange all forms of deceit for truth. Then open your heart to receive the love of God by making a personal confession that Jesus Christ is the risen Savior and invite Him to be Lord over every area of your life. That confession begins a journey of faith, dependency, and trust in the Sovereign God.

Christ died so that you may live and be made alive to live freely in and with Him. Please receive this truth. Why is this important for you to understand now? Because now is the time for you to be and do all that God has called you to be and do. Do not waste another moment living in any form of bondage. Do not continue to live in obscurity or any type of false reality. See beyond your past, beyond your mistakes, failures, and propensity to mess up and fall short. See beyond where you are right now. See and know yourself through the eyes of your Creator and heavenly Father. Why? Because **NOW IS THE TIME FOR LIBERTY!** Now is the time for you to be all you were created and born to be!

WORDS OF ETERNAL LIBERTY

(Read aloud)

Father, God, I am ready to discover my true self in You.
I believe you love me, so I ask you to forgive me for all my sins.
I now believe in my heart and confess with my mouth
that you gave your Son, Jesus, to die on the cross for me
then you raised Him from the dead.
So, I now invite your Son, Jesus, into my life as Lord and Savior.
(St. John 3:16 & Romans 10:9-10)

If you have sincerely prayed this prayer, you are saved,
and you are free!
ABUNDANT LIFE AND ETERNAL LIBERTY
YOU ARE FREE TO BE WHO
GOD HAS CALLED YOU TO BE!!!

LIBERTY FINALLY SPEAKS:

NOW IS THE TIME FOR LIBERTY!

ABOUT THE AUTHOR

Deneen Anderson is CEO of MD Writers' Alliance: A company whose services include manuscript development, editing, transcription, ghostwriting, and publishing services. Deneen has both a master's and bachelor's degree in nursing. She is a Psychiatric Mental Health Nurse Practitioner with over 23 years of clinical service in behavioral health.

Deneen is a licensed and ordained Prophet and minister of the Gospel, an intercessor, and a motivational speaker with a genuine love for God, His Word, and His people.

She is an impassioned teacher who is also the organizer and overseer of Time for Liberty Ministries, a non-denominational fellowship established in 2003 during her residency in Sacramento, California. The ministries' vision and mission are to obtain liberty through a relationship with Christ, through the study of God's word, prayer, and discipleship. The ministry's clarion call to all: **NOW IS THE TIME FOR LIBERTY!**

Deneen Anderson works diligently to fulfill her personal mandate to free others as she has lovingly been freed!

Deneen currently resides in Tinley Park, IL, and is the mother of three adult children, five grandchildren, and three goddaughters.

Contact the author: mdwritersalliance@gmail.com

Printed in the United States
by Baker & Taylor, Publisher Services

Printed in the United States
by Baker & Taylor Publisher Services